How To Make M ClickBank (Even Website)!

By KC Tan – http://websproutacademy.com

Download Your ClickBank Success Kit! 4

Note from the Author 6

Introduction 8

What is ClickBank? 11

3 Reasons Why ClickBank Triumphs Over Other Affiliate Programs 13

Do You Really Need a Website to Make Money With ClickBank? 15

What You Need to Know Before You Make Money with ClickBank 16

ClickBank Direct Linking Strategy – What is Direct Linking? 18

ClickBank Numbers – What You Must Know! 20

How I Use CBengine to Find Products to Promote 23

Choosing The Right ClickBank Products to Promote 26

- a. Types of Products That People Will More Likely Buy Online 26
- b. A Product Sales Page With or Without Videos – Which is Better? 26
- c. Copy & Paste Mastery 27
- d. People Will Only Buy From You If the Product Does This... 28
- e. Do You Know That Search Engines Dislike Pop-Ups? 28

ClickBank Products That You Should Avoid Promoting 30

How to Get a ClickBank Product For Free? 32

Best Traffic Sources for Marketing ClickBank Products 34

Worst Traffic Sources for Marketing ClickBank Products 36

Avoid These Costly Mistakes Made by Newbies! 37

How I Got Over $70 in Sales With Only $4 Investment Using the Direct Linking Strategy 39

Bing Ads Account Creation 41

5 Campaign Creation Secrets That You Must Follow! 43

Proven Keyword Generation Techniques That Your Competitors Don't Know 46

Writing a Winning Advertisement! 52

Tweaking for Greater Sales and Profit! 56

Direct Linking FAQs 59

    Why do I make money on some days but other days I don't? 59

    How do I tell which keywords are not relevant for my campaign when I am doing daily tweaking? 59

    Besides Bing/Yahoo, can I advertise on other search engines? 60

    My Bing Ads account has been deactivated, please help! 60

    It has been more than three days but there are still no clicks in my campaign! 61

    What should I do if I'm still not getting any sales from my campaign? 61

    Can I apply the direct linking strategy to other affiliate programs? 62

    Is it a worthwhile investment to join ClickBank University? 62

    Do you have video tutorials for all the steps in this book? 62

    If I can't generate a stable income through direct linking, what strategy should I use then? 62

How to Create Long Term Income Leveraging ClickBank Products! 64

    Build a List Based On Your Interest 64

    Build a List of Subscribers Based On a Niche, Not a Product 65

Educate More Than You Sell 65

3 Minute Squeeze Page Secrets That No One Tells You! (Creating a Squeeze Page Without Domain and Hosting) 67

Important Tips When Building Your List 69

How to Build a List of Responsive Subscribers? 71

Email #1: Introduce yourself & make an impact! (Day 0) 71

Email #2: Give them a big benefit for subscribing! (Day 2) 72

Email #3: Share a testimonial! (Day 3) 72

Email #4: Give them more information relating to the affiliate product (Day 5) 72

Email #5: Make an offer! (Day 7) 73

Email #6: Remind them of the offer! (Day 8) 73

Email #7: Share with them a useful video! (Day 10) 73

Get Your US$100 Bonus Here! 75

Further Resources 76

Download Your ClickBank Success Kit!

Before you start reading the book, go to the following URL to subscribe to my mailing list to receive the following resources:

- How to identify keywords that will attract people to buy your ClickBank products!
- How to create different keyword matches in seconds!
- How to setup squeeze page without domain name and hosting!
- Regular tips on how to profit from ClickBank!

Get Your Free Gifts At:

http://bitly.com/clickbanksuccesskit

Note from the Author

The goal of this book is to help you to make your first successful affiliate sale in ClickBank (without a website) as quickly as possible. To save you time, I shall skip all the "commonsense" notions and devote this book to explain the practical strategies that have worked for me in making money with ClickBank without a website.

I choose to preserve my own words in this book over engaging a professional editor as I hope that you as the reader can connect with my emotions as I write. I do my very best to ensure all the sentences in this book are clear and easy to read and I hope to have your understanding on any writing imperfections in this book before you begin.

I believe some of you are not new to ClickBank and may have experienced practical challenges making money with ClickBank despite what you have been hearing from others about it. You will soon learn in this book that in every profitable business you need a proper process, as well as the right ingredients – in the right amounts. Most of the people who teach ClickBank share with you merely the process and the ingredients but neglect the specifics of how much is considered "right". In this book, I will reveal to you all the practical essentials that you need to know, which you will be learning towards the second half of this book.

The information in this book is the result of my years of testing and persistence in making money with ClickBank. I am telling you that it *is* possible to make money with ClickBank and many of my students have already done so. There is one common characteristic that I find in all the people who succeed in making money online and that is – **NEVER GIVE UP!** This is also my word of advice to you.

I really hope that you will put the things you learn in this book into action and improve on it along the way. Finding a time in your daily or regular routine that you can devote 100% focus into growing your ClickBank business and staying consistent is key.

I wish you the very best and perhaps someday you can come forward to teach someone else to make money online because you have seen it, worked it and achieved it!

Sincerely,
KC Tan
Living on a beautiful island called Singapore
http://kctan.asia

Introduction

First, I want to thank you for purchasing this book and I believe there is a strong desire in you to make a profit through promoting ClickBank products. You may not be new to ClickBank but what you are about to learn in this book will potentially transform your perspective and the way you look at ClickBank.

The main focus of this book is to show you how to make money by promoting ClickBank products as an affiliate. Please note that this book does not cover how to create a digital product to be sold in the ClickBank marketplace. For this purpose, I would suggest that you take a look at ClickBank University's program.

This book is written primarily for people with an interest in affiliate marketing and want to explore it as a means of making money (without any website). This book is also suitable for people who have tried promoting ClickBank products with little or no results so far.

I have been trying to make money with ClickBank since 2005 and it is only in recent years that I start to see results after spending thousands of dollars online to learn the 'secrets' from others. You see, most people who teach you how to make money online will not tell you how much hard work you need, and often times people jump in with a misunderstanding that it is easy to make money with ClickBank. Thus, it is my responsibility to remind you that the steps taught in this book may be simple but it requires your commitment and effort. It is not just blind copying and pasting, but it is a skill that takes time to hone in order to see sustainable results.

In order to get the most out of this book, you need to first understand the various aspects of ClickBank and types of traffic sources, which I will explain in the first part of this book. I would like to request that you follow my steps exactly (do not attempt to modify the techniques taught in this book) until you make your first sale. Also, please do not skip any section of this book because every page holds information that I spent huge sums of money to learn about and you do not want to miss any part of it. Do yourself a favor as you will be saving yourself valuable resources (time and money) by avoiding those costly mistakes. Read this book as often as you need, you will gain new perspectives every time.

In 2014, I also created an online course teaching people how to make money with ClickBank and I'm grateful that I now have more than 1,500 students from all over the world who have enrolled in my course at the point of writing this book. Now I receive messages from students every other day telling me how happy they are when they receive their first sale in ClickBank! Trust me, the next person will be you – if you don't give up until you see your first sale!

The following are some of the testimonials (unedited) that I received.

"After 14 months buying different courses. I realized getting courses from a Sales person is not quite a good idea since their concerns is to sale. In this course, Kc Tan, as an instructor has put in the effort to teach in a thorough and detailed manner. I was already pleased with the course and it happened. I got a sale. I was very excited and I was not expecting to have one this soon. Thank you for the thorough and detailed lessons. I definitely will recommend this course to anyone who is struggling and wants to see the visual details to how it is done." - Orlando Torres

----

"This is my first Udemy class and I really enjoyed!! Today I got my first sale as following this course. Thank you KC! :)" - Yoko Rodriguez

----

"Hi KC

I got my 1st sales in 2 days (16 clicks). Thank you for this course, It is the easiest for newbie to make money fast." - Phyllis Tang

---

"Thank you KC for being such an effective and quality on-line trainer. I found that all the tips you had given were practical and I benefited from them. I worked through them and within 2 weeks, I already had sales and more than 890 clicks for two products. A winning course.." - Wincom

---

I am blessed to receive positive reviews from people all around the world whenever they receive sales after following the techniques I teach them. Feel free to send me an email to share your joy with me when you make your first sale after applying what you learnt in this book. I look forward to hear from you!

What is ClickBank?

ClickBank is the largest online program that anyone can join to sell or promote digital products (ebooks, videos, audio, graphics, software, etc.). They carry thousands of products on a wide variety of categories ranging from personal development, finance, education, parenting, to skin care, games, cooking, travel and more. In fact you can find products in ClickBank on almost any topic you can think of!

There are two ways to make money with ClickBank. One is to create a digital product and sell it in the marketplace (this aspect will not be covered in this book). Affiliates who help to promote your product and successfully make a sale will be paid a commission based on a rate that is determined by you, the product creator.

The second way is to become an affiliate of ClickBank and promote any of the products in the marketplace for a commission. Most ClickBank products pay a generous commission of between 50% to 75%. This means that as a ClickBank affiliate, you can get a commission of up to 75% for promoting some products! This is a great incentive for affiliates for all the hard work that you do in marketing the products and driving sales for the product creators!

Signing up as a ClickBank affiliate is really easy by following these steps:

1. Go to ClickBank.com and click on the Sign Up link.

2. Fill up the application form using your real name (make sure this name tallies with your bank account name – especially important if you want to receive your commission payment by check).
3. Click the 'Submit' button and you're done!
4. Note down your nickname (this will be your affiliate id).

Upon signing up, you will have your own unique affiliate link for each product. I will show you how to obtain this link later. For now, just be mindful of this important tip. For you to receive commission from ClickBank, the sales has to and must be made through your affiliate link.

3 Reasons Why ClickBank Triumphs Over Other Affiliate Programs

If you are new to Internet marketing and you do not have your own product yet, I'd strongly recommend you to get started as an affiliate with ClickBank. Let me share with you three reasons why ClickBank is the top choice for affiliates and why it is a good platform for you to start your affiliate marketing business.

1. **Instant Approval** – All you need to do is to fill up the application form in ClickBank's website and your account will be created instantaneously! There is no approval process at all. When that is done, you are free to start promoting any product that is listed in the ClickBank marketplace.

2. **Digital Products** – Most ClickBank products are digital which means there is no inventory, packaging and shipping involved. This also implies that buyers can immediately download the product that they have bought without any time lag! This is especially important when you have customers who want to get instant access to information.

3. **Flexible Payout** – Not all affiliate programs can pay you via direct deposit especially if you are not located in United States. For ClickBank, they offer the option of direct deposit (for selected countries outside United States), which makes it really convenient for you to receive payment from them. Besides direct deposit, you can also choose to receive your commission earnings by check. To configure your payment settings, simply login to your ClickBank account and click 'Settings' then edit 'Payment Information'.

Feel free to bookmark this page as this information may come in handy when you're deciding whether other affiliate programs are worthwhile to try!

Do You Really Need a Website to Make Money With ClickBank?

If you have no experience in creating a website or do not fancy doing one for that matter, the answer will be a welcome relief to you: the answer is no!

Having a website is not a must when it comes to making money with ClickBank. As long as you have a means of bringing traffic (web visitors) to the product that you are promoting – which need not necessarily involve a website – you have a business!

Therefore the thing you should focus on is matching the right traffic to the right product. This is a crucial part of the sales conversion process. When you are able to attract the right people to look at the product that you are promoting, you will start to see sales coming your way.

Here are some examples of what makes a good platform-to-product match:

- Promoting a "How to write a resume" product to your LinkedIn contacts;
- Promoting a "How to get rid of back pain" product to people who are searching for "get rid of back pain" in search engines;
- Promoting a photography online course to friends whom you know are interested in learning photography.

Conversely, one of the worst mistakes you can make is to promote a parenting ebook to friends who have yet to become parents! Yes, you get the idea!

What You Need to Know Before You Make Money with ClickBank

Before we begin, I would like to put the record straight about a few things. While making money online with ClickBank is entirely possible, it is not as easy as what it appears to be. Some new ClickBank affiliates assumed that this is a no-brainer business. There are people who are littering their affiliate links on the Internet and expecting sales to come their way. Unfortunately, this is not going to work!

Imagine yourself in the shoes of the customer. If you chanced upon a random product on a website that is of little or no relevance to you, what would you do? Ignore it, yes? Will you bother clicking on the link to find out more? Of course not, you probably don't even remember seeing it!

In a nutshell, how can you get the product that you're promoting to be *seen* by the right people – the people who will be interested enough to notice your product and click on your affiliate link? Besides, for someone to be convinced enough to buy that product, the product needs to either solve a problem for them, or is at least recommended by someone they know or trust. These are important factors that need to be considered and will be discussed in greater detail when you learn about the core technique called the Direct Linking Strategy in the chapters that follow.

There is also no such thing as overnight success when it comes to promoting ClickBank products. It took me years to make a profit but it is my belief that it will take you a much shorter time to make your first sale (and more in the future) if you follow the strategies mapped out in this book.

One final tip I have for you is this – to achieve greater results, always try out the product for yourself before recommending and promoting it to others. Many affiliate marketers are promoting things that they haven't even used before themselves! To me, this makes no practical sense and it will be much more difficult for people to trust you and for what you say. Remember, actions speak louder than words. If you're going to talk the talk, you'd better walk the walk!

ClickBank Direct Linking Strategy – What is Direct Linking?

This chapter explains an overview of the Direct Linking Strategy which is the core technique of this book that will help you to make your first dollar in ClickBank in the quickest time possible. Do read this section as many times as you need to ensure that you understand how direct linking works before moving on with the rest of the chapters.

To make money promoting ClickBank products, you need to attract as many *targeted* customers as you can to look at the products that you are promoting and buy them through your affiliate link. To that end, direct linking works by sending traffic *directly* from search engines to the ClickBank product sales page by means of search engine advertising. This technique is also known as pay-per-click marketing.

Let me illustrate how it works. First, you will want to create advertisements for the ClickBank product that you are promoting. Once that is done, people who are searching for information that is related to the product that you are promoting will see your ad displayed in the search engine results. If he/she clicks on your advertisement (which is embedded with your ClickBank affiliate link), they will be directed to the product sales page straight away. Should they buy the product, you will earn a commission!

This whole process may sound simple but it requires some skill and practice for you to make a profit using this technique. The secret in direct linking is to trigger your advertisement to be shown to people who are searching for *keywords* that are related to the products that you are promoting. For example, if you are promoting a product that helps to reduce hair loss, one of the related keywords you can include in your ad campaign is 'hair loss remedy'. Once you have a campaign that brings you more than what you spend on advertising every day, you have a winning campaign! And this is exactly what I want to help you achieve.

ClickBank Numbers – What You Must Know!

Now that you are clear about where we are headed, it's time to get down to the details! Let's start by taking a look at one of the products in ClickBank to find out what the key metrics of a product are and what those numbers mean. The example that I am using in this chapter is "Linkedinfluence – The Ultimate Linkedin Training Course". To view the actual product, go to the ClickBank marketplace and type in 'LinkedIn course' in the search box.

> **Important Tip**: How do you obtain your affiliate link for a product in ClickBank? It's simple. First, make sure you are logged in to your ClickBank account (this will allow ClickBank to auto-populate your affiliate link). In the marketplace, click on the red 'PROMOTE' button for the product and your affiliate link will be displayed in a pop-up window. Your affiliate link should look something like this:
>
> *http://b0c22grndms02u9joapbh6ucn0.hop.clickbank.net/*

What the numbers mean:

Avg $/sale: This bolded number on the right represents the average amount each affiliate earns for each sale.

This figure is derived based on total affiliate sales over the number of affiliates at this current point in time. Take this number with a pinch of salt to give you a hint of how much on average you will potentially earn per transaction as an affiliate, which is $87.07 for this particular product. Do bear in mind that this may not necessarily be the actual amount that everyone will make!

Initial $/sale: This is the exact amount of money you will earn for each successful sale made through your affiliate link.

For this product, you will be paid $47.65 in commission if someone clicks on your affiliate link and buys the product.

Avg %/Sale: This percentage shows how much of the product sales goes to you in affiliate commission for each successful sale.

In this example, the Avg %/sale is 50% which means you will receive a commission of 50% of the product price when someone buys. Since you also know that this percentage is equivalent to $47.65 in commission, you can estimate the selling price of this product to be $96 approximately.

Avg Rebill Total: This statistic is applicable primarily to products that offer optional membership or subscription services in addition to the core product.

While "Avg $/sale" refers to the average amount an affiliate earns from the sale of the core product, "Avg Rebill Total" represents the average amount an affiliate earns every month from each buyer that also subscribes to the add-on services.

In this example, an Avg Rebill Total of $511.11 means that an affiliate earns an average of $511.11 per month from each buyer that chose to subscribe to the add-on services.

If you come across products that do not have the Avg Rebill Total statistic, it means these are single products that do not come with membership or subscription add-ons. In such cases, the Avg $/sale amount will be the same as the Initial $/sale amount.

Avg % Rebill: This percentage shows how much you will make from the recurring subscription fee of the product.

For example, if the product offers a membership subscription of $100 per month, you will get 50% of the $100, which is $50 every month until the day the person unsubscribes from the program.

Grav: Grav stands for Gravity. What it means is the higher the gravity, the higher the number of purchases the product has received over the recent weeks. If the gravity number is zero, it means that there has been zero sales for the product for several weeks. Gravity is the most important metric to consider when it comes to choosing the right product to promote. We will touch more on gravity in the next chapter.

Before you move on to the following chapter, do take this opportunity to browse around the marketplace for products of your interest and notice the differences in percentages and gravity. What is the highest gravity and Avg %/sale you found?

How I Use CBengine to Find Products to Promote

With thousands of products available in ClickBank for you to choose from, which ones should you promote? Learning to choose the right product to promote is one of the key components to success so let's get your first step right!

As mentioned in the earlier chapter, the most important metric you need to look at when selecting a product is its *gravity*. One general rule of thumb is to avoid products with zero gravity, in other words, products with no sales for the past weeks. If conversion for such products have been miserable – whether it's due to poorly written sales copy or other reasons – you certainly don't want to be wasting your time and budget on promoting them.

In order for you to choose from the thousands of products available in ClickBank according to their gravity, let me share with you a useful tool (it's free!) that can help you to easily compare the gravity of all products!

CBengine.com is a very user-friendly tool that not only shows you the full list of products in ClickBank at a glance, it also allows you to sort the products by gravity in a matter of seconds!

The following steps detail how you can use CBengine to obtain a list of ClickBank products sorted by gravity:

1. Go to cbengine.com.
2. Click on the 'Browse' tab at the top right of the page.
3. Select a category that you are interested in. For instance, the 'Health' category.
4. The full list of products in the selected category will be shown. Click on the 'Averages' link at the top of the page (under Regroup Results By). This will trigger the results to be displayed in table form.

5. Now the final step is to sort the products by gravity in descending order. To do that, simply click on the 'Gravity' header <u>twice</u> (clicking the header once will sort the list in ascending order and clicking a second time will sort the list in descending order).

As a start, I would recommend you to choose a product with **gravity between 1 to 60**. For instance, you can consider "The Kidney Disease Solution" which has a gravity of 37 (at the time of writing).

It is best to avoid products with very high gravity (like the ones shown above) for now as there are a lot of affiliates who are already promoting these products and it is extremely competitive to get sales.

Besides gravity, what are the other important factors that you need to take note of in selecting a good ClickBank product to promote? Read on to find out more in the next chapter.

Choosing The Right ClickBank Products to Promote

After you have filtered the list of products based on gravity (between 1 to 60), the following key factors will further help you in choosing a suitable ClickBank product to promote using the direct linking strategy.

This is one of the most important, if not the most important, chapter in this entire book so be sure to re-read this section as many times as you need!

   a. **Types of Products That People Will More Likely Buy Online**

If you do not have a specific category of products that you want to promote, you can consider choosing products from the following categories where people generally have a higher propensity to buy online.

1. Health – Any product or information that can help to treat or cure an illness or disease.
2. Make Money – Any product that helps people in the area of business or make money online.
3. Self Help – Any product that helps to improve oneself, such as increase self-confidence, stop procrastination, develop leadership skills, time management.

   b. **A Product Sales Page With or Without Videos – Which is Better?**

The technique that you'll be learning in this book is called the direct linking method, which involves sending prospects from your advertisement directly to the ClickBank product that you are promoting.

Under such circumstances, you are dealing with people who are looking for quick online solutions to their problems and they do not necessarily have the time and patience to finish watching an entire video to know what is it that you have to offer.

Therefore, do not select a product that has only a video on their sales page! It's a good practice to always choose a product with a sales page that contains text write-up. A product that has both video and text write-up on the sales page works fine too.

While video-only sales page is good, it is not ideal for direct linking strategy. Do bear this in mind.

c. Copy & Paste Mastery

Especially for beginners, I do not encourage you to waste time on trying to write your own advertisements, at least at the beginning stage. It takes time to hone your copywriting skills to be able to write effective copies that bring conversion. Hence I'd suggest you to gain maximum leverage by choosing products that provide **ready resources for affiliates (look out for advertisement templates especially)**.

There are two ways to find out whether a product offers affiliate resources.

First, look at the product description - some product creators will include a special url for affiliates to download templates and resources.

If the affiliate resource link cannot be found in the product description, go to the product sales page itself and look for a link called 'Affiliates'. Most ClickBank product sales pages have one and it is usually located at the footer area.

d. People Will Only Buy From You If the Product Does This...

Remember, any product that can solve a problem is a good product.

How the direct linking method works is when your prospects click on your advertisement, they are brought directly to the sales page of the product that you are promoting. At that instant, one of the key factors that affects the prospects' decision to buy (or don't buy) is the fundamental question of whether that product solves an urgent problem for the person.

If the product that you are promoting does not solve an urgent problem, it will be very difficult to have conversions. So, always be sure to choose a product that addresses an urgent need, such as solving a health problem, if you want to make money using direct linking.

e. Do You Know That Search Engines Dislike Pop-Ups?

Another important consideration is to select products with a sales page that does not show pop-ups when a visitor leaves the page. As we are using search engines to advertise the ClickBank products, we need to adhere to their policies that disallow advertisements on webpages that trigger pop-ups upon exit. Thus in choosing a product, make it a habit to visit the sales page first to check if there are pop-ups when you close the window. If there is, then this is not a suitable product to promote using the direct linking method.

ClickBank Products That You Should Avoid Promoting

Firstly, avoid forex trading products. Many people are tempted to promote forex related products as they offer generous commissions to affiliates. However, many affiliates that promoted forex trading software products end up with reports of high refund rates. Hence my suggestion is to stay away from ClickBank products that are related to forex trading, especially if you are new to ClickBank.

Secondly, avoid choosing products whose sales pages contain other advertisements. When browsing for products in ClickBank, you may come across sales pages that look like a blog or worst yet, display other advertisements that lead visitors to other pages and distract their attention away from the core product. Therefore, be careful not to choose such products with poorly designed sales pages as they usually result in low conversions.

Thirdly, if you are someone who is new to affiliate marketing and PPC (pay-per-click) marketing, you do not want to start off by choosing a product that does not offer any affiliate resources. The benefit of having these ready resources (such as banners, email templates, PPC advertisement samples, etc.) is that it gives you a much faster head start towards success. If you don't have access to these resources, imagine having to create everything from scratch!

Finally, I do not promote ClickBank products with rating of less than 3 (out of 5) stars in CBengine.com. You can click on a product in CBengine to check the rating of that product. The suggested rating of a good product to promote is 3 stars and above.

How to Get a ClickBank Product For Free?

If you want to get a copy of any ClickBank product for free to test before you promote it, the best way to do this legitimately is to request one from the product creator directly. Of course, you need to do this with tact so that the chances of you getting your free copy will be higher! Here's what I'd recommend you to do.

First, recognize that all product creators share the same objective. They want more sales for their products. If you can show them that you are capable of contributing to that end – that is help them to sell more of their products – I believe they would be more than happy to offer you their support! In this case, giving you a free copy of the product doesn't cost them additional money too.

Below is an actual email that I sent to a product creator in ClickBank who then gave me a free copy of his product subsequently. The important thing here is to keep your message short and concise – start off with a self-introduction and share how you intend to help the product creator to get more sales after you receive a copy of his product.

Hi [product creator's name],

This is KC and I am one of the affiliates of ClickBank.

I came across your product – [product name] in ClickBank and would like to promote it using PPC (Bing Ads) as I have allocated some budget to advertise every month. I'd like to request for a copy of your product to review so I can recommend it to my friends through social media as well.

I look forward to your reply and attached is a screenshot of my recent sales for other ClickBank products that I promote. Thank you!

Regards
KC

Do note that the last sentence in the email template is completely optional. If you have proof of recent sales that you made from promoting other products, great - remember to attach the relevant screenshot in your email. Otherwise you can leave the last line out in your email.

Just a word of caution: bear in mind that sometimes no matter how hard you try, there are product creators who will ignore your request. Don't get upset, just move on then!

Best Traffic Sources for Marketing ClickBank Products

After selecting a product to promote, the next step is to bring *targeted* visitors to the product sales page. By targeted visitors, I'm referring to people who are specifically searching for a product or solution for their needs.

Before I elaborate further, let me introduce an important marketing concept to you below.

Inbound Marketing VS Outbound Marketing

All marketing activities can be classified as either inbound or outbound.

Outbound marketing refers to the act of reaching out to people to get customers. The following are some common outbound marketing methods:

- Distributing flyers
- Newspaper advertisement
- Cold calling

In contrast, a more effective approach for businesses (including online businesses) is inbound marketing where customers voluntarily come forward to look for you rather than you chasing after them. Some great examples of inbound marketing include:

- Search engine marketing
- Word of mouth

The direct linking technique that I will be teaching in this book is an *inbound* marketing strategy.

Essentially, it leverages the power of Search engine marketing (also known as Pay-Per-Click) to direct highly targeted leads to your product. Imagine you are promoting a product that helps to lower blood pressure. Someone who is looking for a solution to his high blood pressure problem goes online to search for "how to lower blood pressure" and sees your advertisement in the search engine results. He finds it relevant and clicks on your advertisement to find out more – this is what I call a targeted visitor with desire! In this book, I will teach you exactly how to implement this strategy.

Besides Pay-Per-Click, another powerful online marketing technique that I recommend is Email marketing, which works especially well for conversions when you send regular informative emails to people whom you know or to your mailing list subscribers. In fact, this method is more effective and cost-efficient than Pay-Per-Click in the long term and I will be covering this in the later part of this book.

Worst Traffic Sources for Marketing ClickBank Products

Now let's take a look at some of the worst traffic sources to avoid using for purposes of promoting ClickBank products.

First, avoid Pay-Per-View traffic. This type of traffic works by you pay when someone visit a website and it popup your advertisement. This method is also known as interruptive marketing. And as you may imagine, the visitors to a particular website almost will not expect to see your website popup, so it is a waste of money if you want to get buyers.

Second, avoid buying automated traffic that guarantees you few thousands visitors at very cheap price ($5 or so)! What I have discovered is that this traffic is often triggered by bots and since they are bots, you will not see any sales! When buying traffic, you have to find out what type of traffic is that and are they targeted?

Third, avoid paying for services such as directories submission or search engine submissions. These techniques are for affiliates who run their own websites. Since we are using direct linking, we do not need these submission services. If you have a website in future, consider submitting your website to directories as this will help search engines to discover your sites and get it ranked. As for search engine submissions, you do not need it nowadays as search engines are very smart and is able to discover your site if you submit it to directories alone.

Avoid These Costly Mistakes Made by Newbies!

In my experience teaching people about making money with ClickBank, I observe some common mistakes that students frequently make which you should avoid at any cost. I hope learning from others' mistakes and taking away these important lessons will help you get started on the right track in the pursuit of your goals.

Number one – Do not choose a product *solely* for the high commission it pays. This is the most common mistake made by people who are new to ClickBank.

In choosing a ClickBank product to promote, you may be tempted to go for the ones that offer the highest commissions to affiliates but this move is a big no-no! If you base your decision solely on the amount of commission you'll get, you are overlooking the other important aspects to consider in choosing a product that is *suitable* for you to promote.

To be able to promote any product effectively, you need to first understand the product itself (what it does, what benefits it brings, etc.). The lack of knowledge or interest in that product will prove it difficult for you to scale your promotion campaigns in the long run and will only jeopardize your chances of success. So, choose your first product wisely – a good place to start is to always follow your interests or topics that you have some knowledge in!

Number two – Do not follow in the footsteps of people who make repeated attempts to buy and refund products in ClickBank just to get products for free. This is another huge mistake! ClickBank strictly condemns such behavior and they will take the necessary actions to ban your account forever. If you really want to get a free copy of a product to try before promoting it, refer to the earlier chapter on how I obtain some ClickBank products for free in a legitimate way.

One last piece of advice I have for you is never try to use false claims to boost conversions! If you are promoting a product that helps people to make money online, never ever lie to people about your earnings if you are not truly making that amount! This principle applies to all types of products. If you want to improve your conversions, try the product personally before you promote it. The best endorsement you can give is an honest one that comes from your heart and based on your genuine experiences. This is a timeless and ageless principle in affiliate marketing.

How I Got Over $70 in Sales With Only $4 Investment Using the Direct Linking Strategy

In the chapters that follow, I will be revealing to you the exact steps on how to put the direct linking strategy into practice. But before we dive into action, let's take a quick look at the actual results that I've gotten from using this technique!

The following webpage (Video 13) shows the proof I generate more than $70 sales with only $4 investment.

https://www.udemy.com/making-money-with-clickbank/?couponCode=website

The above results are what I have personally experienced after applying the direct linking strategy, *but* this does not serve as a limit to what you can attain! In fact many of my students around the world have already surpassed me to achieve better results for themselves. If you would follow the principles I share in this book and put it into practice, you will see positive results eventually.

Are you ready to get into action? Let's begin!

Bing Ads Account Creation

To recap, direct linking involves the use of pay-per-click advertising to attract people who are searching for a particular solution in search engines and directing them to the ClickBank product that you are promoting when they click on your advertisement.

Therefore the first thing you need to do is to create a Bing Ads account (if you do not already have one) so that you can start to create campaigns to advertise your chosen ClickBank products on Bing/Yahoo.

You may ask me, why should we use Bing, and not Google since the latter is more popular and has more traffic? Here's why I chose Bing Ads over Google AdWords:

- It is much cheaper to advertise in Bing Ads than in Google AdWords. Bidding gets extremely competitive in Google AdWords so it typically costs more than $1 per click, but with Bing Ads you can get clicks for as little as 5 cents per click!
- Bing Ads is more affiliate friendly; you can do direct linking in Bing Ads whereas direct linking is not allowed in Google AdWords.
- When you advertise in Bing Ads, your advertisements will show up in not one, but two search engines – both Bing and Yahoo!

Overall, it is much easier to make a profit by using Bing Ads since lower costs implies greater margin for profits!

When you're ready to register a Bing Ads account, go to http://advertise.bingads.microsoft.com/en-us/sign-up and click the 'Sign Up' button. On the next page, select 'Use existing Microsoft account' if you have an existing Microsoft account, otherwise select the 'Create a new Microsoft account' option. Click

'Continue' and follow the onscreen instructions to complete registration.

Note that one of the steps of the registration process requires you to create a new ad campaign. At this point in time, all you need to do is enter dummy information into the new campaign and upon successful account creation, you can simply delete the dummy campaign anytime.

In addition, you will need to add a payment method to allow Bing to bill you for the clicks you receive for your ads. You can choose between the prepay (pay now) or postpay (pay later) options. Prepay means you will deposit money into your Bing Ads account and your advertising costs will be deducted from the balance, while postpay means Bing will charge your debit/credit card every time your account reaches the billing threshold. There is no best method, it all depends on your personal preference. However keep in mind that you can't change the setting once you have selected it.

5 Campaign Creation Secrets That You Must Follow!

Congratulations! Once your Bing Ads account is set up, the next step is to create an ad campaign!

Before we proceed further, make sure you have selected a product from ClickBank that you want to start promoting. If you have yet to decide on one, you can refer to the earlier chapters on how to use CBengine to choose a good product to promote. Come back again after you have selected at least one product.

Once you have your product(s), you are ready to create your first campaign! Login to your Bing Ads account and click on the 'Create Campaign' link. You will see a list of fields that you need to fill in. Most of these fields are pretty standard but I want to share a few knacks with you that will make a difference between a winning and a losing ad campaign.

First, avoid allocating a high daily budget for your ad campaign whenever you are promoting a product for the first time. Your daily budget refers to how much you want to spend on your ads every day. When you are first starting to promote a product, this is the time for you to test out the demand and conversion of the product – how high is the ad click rate and how much sales you are getting – so you want to control your advertising spending to keep your risks in check. A reasonable daily budget that I'd suggest is between US$3 to US$5 for a start (if you allocate a budget of $3 a day, that already works out to a total spending of about $90 per month for one campaign).

Some people ask me if it is alright to allocate a lower daily budget. My answer is yes, you can start off with a lower daily budget and adjust it along the way when your campaign becomes profitable. However do note that a lower daily budget means that you will be getting relatively lesser clicks and as a result, it will take a longer time for you to see the results of your campaign.

The second tip is also related to budgeting options, particularly how quickly to spend your daily budget. By default, Bing distributes your daily budget to be spent evenly throughout the day. My recommendation is to set your ad delivery to accelerated pacing instead (select the 'Accelerated' option under Daily Budget Options). This option tells Bing to show your ads as often as possible from the start of the day so you can max out your daily budget as quickly as possible.

One advantage of choosing the daily accelerated budget option is that you will have a better chance of maximizing the number of clicks you can get with your daily budget as compared to the default option. The more clicks you get in a shorter time, the faster you can get a sale! Furthermore, setting the accelerated budget option allows you to test out the online demand of your product's niche. If your daily budget is maxed out very quickly at the early part of the day, it shows that the volume of searches for the keywords in your niche is high and this is a positive indicator that you can further scale your campaign moving forward.

The third knack is to specify *only* United States and United Kingdom as the targeting countries of your ad campaign. Based on my experience, targeting these two countries have brought the highest conversion rates for my campaigns and it is not surprising as people living in U.S. and UK generally have a higher propensity to purchase things online. Focusing your marketing efforts on these two countries for a start is the quickest way for you to see conversions. If you want to target other countries as well, I would suggest that you create a separate campaign for those countries so you can have a comparison of the results!

After you have specified your targeting countries (say U.S. and UK), the next important location setting you must remember is to select 'Show ads to people in your targeted location' (under Advanced Location Options). This setting serves to tighten your campaign to ensure that your ads are shown only to people *located* in the targeting countries of your campaign (i.e. only people living in U.S. and UK) – not to people who are searching *about* the countries. This setting has saved me thousands of dollars in advertising! I've had students who experienced low conversions only to realize that they have forgotten to set this option correctly!

Next, avoid setting overly high keyword bids at the start! Bid refers to the amount that you are willing to pay for every click that your ad receives. If you set your bids too high, you may risk incurring unnecessary losses. For a start, a good rule of thumb is to set a bid equivalent to 1% (or less) of your affiliate commission for that product. On average, one can expect to get a sale for every 100 clicks to your ad so following the rule will ensure that you will break even at the minimum. For example, if the product that you are promoting gives you US$25 in commission for each sale, you should put your bid rate as US$0.25 per click at the maximum. Should you receive one sale after 100 clicks (which cost you US$25), you could at least break even! But trust me, if you have a tight and well-tweaked campaign, you will get sales in far less than 100 clicks!

Finally, you can choose to display your ads on two types of networks in Bing Ads –search network and content network. For the direct linking strategy, we will be using only search network (showing your ads on search sites) as it is more targeted than content network (showing your ads on content websites). Even though you're not using content network for your campaign, Bing still requires you to enter bids for both networks. What I always do is to simply enter a bid of US$0.01 bid for the content network and that will do the trick.

Proven Keyword Generation Techniques That Your Competitors Don't Know

A lot of beginners often overlook the importance of building a strong keyword list for their ad campaign. One common mistake is that people have the tendency to think of keywords on the fly and create their list based on random words or phrases that come to mind. Due to lack of a proper system, most people often end up with less than 100 keywords in their campaign and soon they would come to a realization that their campaign is receiving too little clicks to see any conversion!

In this chapter, I will teach you techniques that will allow you to generate at least 1,000 to 2,000 targeted keywords for your first campaign. This will give you an edge over most of your competitors. It is only with a sizable number of keywords that you will have better chances of launching a winning ad campaign. Remember, the more keywords you have running in your campaign, the higher the chances that your ad will show up on the search engines.

Besides quantity, another critical success factor involves filtering your list for keywords that are of high relevance to your product so that you are attracting the right people to look at your ads. Read on to learn the steps to build your power keyword list!

Using the Google Keyword Planner

The best tool that I would recommend you to use for generating your keyword list is the Google Keyword Planner. What the Google Keyword Planner does is it tells you how many people are searching for a particular keyword (in Google) and better still, it suggests to you a whole list of other related keywords that people are currently searching for! The idea here is to leverage Google's actual data to tell us the exact keywords that people are searching for and use it for our campaign in Bing Ads. This will allow you to have a good list of keywords to start with while saving loads of time!

In the following paragraphs, I will share with you tips on how to use the Google Keyword Planner effectively to generate your keyword list. To help you visualize the steps better, I have also created a tutorial video to demonstrate how to use this tool in step by step format. You will receive this video as a free resource when you sign up for my mailing list (near the beginning of this book)!

First, let's go to https://adwords.google.com/KeywordPlanner (alternatively you can google for 'google keyword planner'). You will need a Gmail account to access the Google Keyword Planner. If you do not have an existing Gmail account, please go to gmail.com to register an account first. Once you have logged in to the Keyword Planner using your Gmail account, select the 'Search for new keyword and ad group ideas' option.

Now you are ready to start generating your keyword list! First, make sure that you edit the default location setting to specify United States as your targeting location. This will remove keywords that are searched by people located outside U.S.. The reason why we choose to look at people in U.S. specifically is because the data is the best representation of search patterns across the world.

Next, think about a general keyword that describes what problem the ClickBank product that you are promoting helps people to solve. For example, 'reduce hair loss', 'lower high blood pressure', etc. Enter the keyword into the 'Your product or service' text field and hit the 'Get ideas' button.

Once the page is refreshed, you will see two tabs: 'Ad group ideas' and 'Keyword ideas'. Select the 'Keyword ideas' tab. Here you'll see that, based on the keyword that you entered earlier, the tool now returns you a comprehensive list of other related keywords that people are also searching for in Google! There are as many as 800 keywords provided (over 20 pages of them) as you scroll right to the bottom of the page. To help you manage this list more efficiently, let's click on the 'Avg monthly searches' header to order the list by search volume so that the keywords with the highest search volumes are sorted nicely at the start of the list.

Next, you want to fine-tune your list by removing keywords that are not relevant to the ClickBank product you are promoting or do not indicate a buying intention. Remember, your primary objective is to attract people to *buy* the product that you are promoting, so by excluding ineffective keywords you are making sure that you are targeting your ads only at people who are most interested in your product.

For instance, if you are promoting a hair loss remedy product, 'hair surgery' and 'hair loss in dogs' are some examples of keywords that are irrelevant to the product that you are promoting and these should be excluded. You also do not want your ad to be shown to people who are searching for 'free hair loss tips'! 'Free' is one of the common words that you should always exclude from your keyword list as the chances of getting a sale from someone who is looking for free things online is almost zero. Similarly, keywords like 'hair loss photos' and 'causes of hair loss' signal that these people are looking for something else and will not be interested in the product that you are offering them so these should be excluded as well.

You need to use your own discretion to decide whether a keyword should be excluded from your keyword list or not. Many people tend to struggle with this phase, so my suggestion to you is – whenever in doubt as to whether a keyword is relevant or not, you can safely remove them.

As you go through the list and identify keywords that you want to remove, simply enter them into the 'Negative Keywords' box on the left, one per line (hit enter to go to the next line). All keywords containing the negative keyword will then be automatically removed from the list. It is a good practice to sift through at least the first five pages of your list to pick up any negative keywords so that your ad campaign will be as targeted as possible.

Once that is done, click on the 'download' button to export the updated keyword list as Excel CSV file and save it in your computer.

Second round of filtering

Open the downloaded CSV file in Microsoft Excel and you should be able to see your full list of keywords. Comb through the list again to check for any negative keywords (keywords that are irrelevant or do not indicate a buying intent) that you may have missed out earlier and delete them. Doing a thorough check will help you save advertising costs on keywords that will not give you any returns!

Creating different keyword matches

After two rounds of filtering, you would now have a smaller list of keywords as compared to the one that was first generated from the Google Keyword Planner. Maybe you are down to 300 to 600 keywords, it doesn't matter. Now we are going to triple the size of your list!

To get started, let me first introduce the different keyword match types – broad, phrase and exact match. Any keyword that you add into your campaign can be assigned any of these match types by means of enclosing the keyword with special symbols. Keyword match types essentially allow you to tell Bing Ads how closely you want a search term to match your keyword in order for your ad to be shown.

For keywords assigned with broad match type, as long as any word in your keyword occurs – in any order – in the search term entered, Bing will show your ad. For instance, if you have *hair loss remedy* as a broad match keyword in your campaign, your ad will be triggered when someone searches for *remedy for hair loss*, *losing hair* or *leg hair remedy how to*. Bing Ads will automatically assign any keyword that is not enclosed with special symbols as broad match type. Likewise, the current list of the keywords that you are working on (extracted from Google Keyword Planner) will also be recognized as broad match when you add them to your Bing Ads campaign.

For phrase match type, Bing will trigger your ad when the full string of your keyword, in that exact same order, is found in the search term. For example, if your keyword is "hair loss remedy", your ad will be shown to people who are searching for *cheap hair loss remedy* or *hair loss remedy for women*. However, search terms like *hair remedy* or *remedy for hair loss* will not trigger your ad because Bing did not detect these three words "hair loss remedy" in this same order in the search term! How you assign a keyword as phrase match in Bing Ads is by enclosing the keyword with double quotes "". An example of phrase match keyword is "hair loss remedy".

The third type of keyword match is straightforward. As the name implies, exact match means the search term entered must have a 100% match with your keyword – with no other words in between, before or after – for your ad to show. If your keyword is [hair loss remedy], Bing will only show your ad when someone searches for *hair loss remedy*; no other search term variations will trigger your ad. Keywords enclosed with [] will be set as exact. An example of exact match keyword is [hair loss remedy].

Having understood all three types of keyword matches, you'll find that at one extreme, broad match gives you the widest audiences reach while compromising on relevance. At the other extreme, exact match offers the highest relevance but it allows you to reach out to a smaller audience. Therefore our plan is to leverage each of their strengths by including all three match types in your Bing Ads campaign. This will boost your keyword list tremendously and give you a strong edge over your competitors.

Using Jumbokeyword.com

From your current list of broad match keywords, you now need to generate two other similar lists for phrase and exact match by adding the relevant special symbols to each keyword. It will be crazy to do this manually so let me suggest the following tool to help you achieve maximum efficiency!

Jumbokeyword.com is an online tool that will help you to complete the job in seconds! All you have to do is to copy all your keywords and paste it into the tool and in a click of a button, it will generate all three keyword match types for you. It's really easy to use and there are instructions provided on the website. But in case you need more guidance, do sign up for my mailing list to receive the step-by-step video!

Once you have your full keyword list containing broad, phrase and exact match types, go ahead and add all the keywords into your campaign in Bing Ads.

Writing a Winning Advertisement!

Have you gotten all your keywords into Bing Ads? Great! You are now just one step away from launching your campaign, and that is to create your ads.

A well-written ad will attract people to click on it and visit the product sales page, so doing this right is extremely crucial to the success of your campaign. This section will cover the essential points on how to create an attention-grabbing ad so that you can attract more targeted visitors to take a look at the ClickBank product that you are promoting.

First, let me share with you the different components of an ad:

- **Ad Title:** The headline has one main objective that is to grab the attention of the person and entice them to read your ad description. You can enter up to 25 characters for the ad title.

- **Ad Description:** The purpose of the ad description is to get people to click on your ad and direct them to the product that you are promoting! You can enter up to 71 characters into the description field.

- **Display URL:** The display URL is the link that will be displayed in your ad.

- **Destination URL:** The destination URL is the webpage that people will be directed to when they click on your ad. Note that the destination URL will *not* be shown in your ad and it need not be the same as your Display URL.

Leverage existing ad templates

I highly encourage you to make use of existing advertisement templates, if any, that are provided by product creators for affiliates. Most of these templates have been tested and proven for conversions so always leverage existing resources first rather than create your own from scratch. Not only will it save you time, it gives you an idea about what works!

Personally, I like to modify the templates slightly by changing a few words here and there as I do not want my ads to be identical to that of other affiliate marketers. That said, it is entirely your call as to whether you want to use the original template as it is or modify it for your purpose.

Use Google as a reference for creating ads

Regardless of what product you are promoting, this technique will supply you with practical ideas on what to write for your own ad. Make use of this method to help you get started especially if the product that you're promoting doesn't provide ready advertisement templates for your use.

Before you write your ad, go to Google.com and enter a keyword that you're targeting. For instance, if you are promoting a product that cures hair loss, you can search for *hair loss remedy*. In the search results returned by Google, you'll notice that there are paid ads displayed at the top of the page as well as in the column on the right.

These ads that you see in Google are created by other advertisers. Take a good look at how they write their ads; these are powerful templates for you to reference and create your own. Please make sure that you do not copy others' ads wholesale; always modify and adapt the ads to suit your targeted audience!

Manage expectations when writing ads

A common mistake that people often make is to write an ad title that is inconsistent with the message conveyed in the product sales page. Look at it from the perspective of your customer – if you see an ad with the headline *Hair Loss Remedy* and after clicking on the ad, you are directed to a page with the title "Sign Up For Our Mailing List Now!", would you take a second look at the webpage? Trust me, most people will not hesitate to leave the page immediately. It is a costly mistake to lose a lead that you have paid for just like that.

To maximize the number of people who will stay on the product page and eventually buy the product that you are promoting, it is of paramount importance to ensure that the ad title is as closely relevant to the title of the sales page as possible.

In addition, you have learnt from the earlier chapters to avoid promoting a product with a video-only sales page. If you really have to choose such a product, my advice to you is to include the word 'video' in your ad headline so that people are expecting to watch a video when they click on your ad. However, my experiences have shown that the word 'video' generally receive lower click rates for ads.

Include a call to action in the ad description

Your ad description should make people want to click on the ad to find out more and one of the most effective ways to achieve that is to include a call to action!

The following are some call to action examples that you can include in your ad description:

- Sign up now!
- Join now!
- Find out more!
- Learn the secrets!

- Access exclusive information!
- Learn how you can do the same now!

Make your ad more readable

A good ad is one that is easy to scan and read, so avoid using jargons that not everyone can understand. In addition, capitalize every word in your ad – the ad title, ad description and even the display URL – to make it more readable. For example, *Cure Hair Loss In A Week* is better than *Cure hair loss in a week*. Instead of *http://hairlossremedy.com*, enter *http://HairLossRemedy.com* as your display URL instead. Notice the difference?

Always do split testing!

It is always a good practice to create at least two ads when setting up a new ad campaign. Bing will show both your ads and tell you how well each performs. By analyzing the click-through-rate (CTR) of each ad, you will be able to determine which one attracted more people to click on it. You can then pause the other ad and create a new one to continue testing.

The following are the ad elements that you can vary and test. Always remember to change one element at a time so that you can have a fair comparison:

- Ad title - Replace your ad title with alternative words that appeal more to your target market.
- Ad description - Test out different call to actions statements.
- Display URL - Try a different display url to see whether it increases the CTR.

Tweaking for Greater Sales and Profit!

After you have created your campaign in Bing Ads, make it a habit to review your campaign regularly and fine-tune it further so that you are continuously improving your ROI (return on investment). Let me share with you the things that I do on a daily and weekly basis which you can follow to get the most out of your Bing Ads campaign!

Daily Campaign Tweaking!

When you are reviewing your campaign every day, one of the key information you need to analyze is the list of keywords that brought you clicks to your ads the day before. There are two things you need to do with this list.

First, look at each of the keywords and assess the quality of traffic you're getting – will someone who's searching for this keyword be interested to look at the product that you are promoting? If yes, keep the keywords running in your campaign. However if you find any keyword that is not as relevant or targeted to the product that you are promoting, you should delete it from your campaign. Though we had done two initial rounds of filtering during the preparation of your keyword list, this step is still necessary to further improve keyword relevance, and optimize your spending only on those keywords that will help to attract the right people to look at the product sales page.

Second, you need to adjust the bid for each keyword so as to optimize the ranking of your ads. Generally the higher the bid entered for a keyword, the higher will be the position of your ad on the search engine results. Ideally you should target for an average position of between 2 to 5. The number one position is not always the most ideal as it typically requires you to invest much more (relative to the second and third position) and it may not be the most cost-efficient. So what I usually do is that I raise/lower each keyword bid accordingly until it reaches an optimal average position of between 2 to 5.

Some keywords will have a delivery status of 'Below first page bid'. This means that Bing is suggesting you to increase the bid rate for the keyword in order for your ad to be shown on the first page of the search results. You can find out what is the suggested bid by clicking on the [...] icon next to the 'Below first page bid' status. If the suggested bid is too high (more than three times your current bid), you may want to consider pausing the keyword first.

Next, you should check whether your campaign daily budget was maxed out for the previous day. If your daily budget was spent to the maximum, what you need to do is either increase your daily budget (if your budget allows) or reduce the bid for the keywords that received clicks. This will ensure that you are maximizing the number of clicks that you are getting to your ads every day.

Your final task of the day is to check whether you received any new sales by logging in to your ClickBank account and accessing your sales report!

Important Weekly Tweaking!

On top of your daily tweaks, do the following every week to ensure that you have a successful campaign overtime!

Firstly, you should evaluate the performance of each of your ads by doing a comparison of their CTR (click-through-rate). CTR is a percentage that is derived based on the number of clicks an ad receives over the number of times the ad is shown. A CTR of 5% means that for every 100 people that saw the ad, 5 people have clicked on it. Hence, the higher the CTR, the more effective is the ad in drawing people to click on it and the better it is!

For instance, assume there are two ads in your campaign, ad A and ad B. In the past week, Ad A delivered a CTR of 10% (10 clicks out of 100 views) while Ad B's CTR was 7.5% (15 clicks out of 200 views). In this case, ad A is the better performing ad since it has a higher CTR than ad B. Therefore I would suggest that you delete ad B, and at the same time, create a new ad (that is different from both ads A and B in title or description). This way, you can test the performance of the new ad against ad A in the following week. Do note in this example that even though ad B received more clicks than ad A (15 vs 10 clicks), ad B is still deemed to have performed worse than ad A because it has a lower CTR. A higher number of clicks doesn't equate to a better ad, so always look at the CTR when deciding which ad to delete.

The second thing you need to do every week is to check whether your campaign is profitable or making you losses! In order to have a profitable campaign, you should have an average of at least one sale per week. And your total spending in Bing Ads should not exceed the amount of money that you make from ClickBank.

Special Note:

Direct linking is an effective method that helps you to see results quickly but in the long term, I do not recommend that you rely on this strategy alone. Read the FAQs in the following chapter to find out more and in the rest of this book, I will teach you another strategy that gives you long term recurring income from ClickBank.

Direct Linking FAQs

Below you'll find answers to the most popular questions that I receive from my students from around the world regarding making money with ClickBank. I hope these will help address some of the questions you have in mind as well!

Why do I make money on some days but other days I don't?

It is normal for sales results to be unpredictable especially if you're using only the direct linking strategy, and no other methods, to promote ClickBank products. The reason is simple – it is a make-or-break scenario. You only have *one* chance to make a sale, which is the moment when someone lands on the product sales page after clicking on your ad. If everything goes well and they buy the product on the spot, you earn a commission! But if they decide to leave the website without buying (which happens), your commission goes down the drain.

Using direct linking, you can expect an average of about one to two sales for every 100 visitors that click on your ad. While I have students who are receiving an average of one sale per week, there are also people who get sales every other day with direct linking.

How do I tell which keywords are not relevant for my campaign when I am doing daily tweaking?

Every day, you just need to focus on keywords that received clicks (to your ads) on the previous day. You can do this easily by specifying the period as yesterday from the top right dropdown box and click on the 'Clicks' header to order the keyword list so that all the keywords that received clicks yesterday will be sorted at the beginning of the list.

Say you're promoting a hair loss product and the keywords that received clicks the day before are :

- Hair loss remedy
- Hair restoration
- Hair loss treatment
- Hair loss causes
- Hair loss photos

Can you determine which keywords are not relevant for the product? In my opinion, all the above are relevant except 'hair loss causes' and 'hair loss photos'.

Besides Bing/Yahoo, can I advertise on other search engines?

You won't be able to do direct linking in Google AdWords as it's not allowed. Besides, it is more expensive to advertise on Google AdWords so I wouldn't recommend it especially if you are new to pay-per-click marketing.

Apart from Bing/Yahoo, you can try this search and display network called 7search.com. The quality of the traffic may not be as high as that of Bing/Yahoo but you can definitely give it a try since the bid rate is cheaper than Bing.

My Bing Ads account has been deactivated, please help!

There could be a few reasons why your Bing account is deactivated. If your account is new, it could be due to security reasons. The first thing you should do is to email Bing support to find out more. I have had a few students who encountered this but managed to resolve all their issues after contacting Bing support.

If your account is not a new one, it could be an issue of violation of Bing Ads guidelines, such as promoting a product with exit pop-ups. The best way to resolve this is to contact Bing support for assistance and work with them to do the necessary changes.

It has been more than three days but there are still no clicks in my campaign!

It is common to take up to three days for your ads to be approved, especially if your Bing Ads account is new. If you still do not receive clicks after three days, you need to check your keywords to see if there are any impressions (the number of times your ad has been shown). If there are impressions but no clicks, this signals that you need to improve your ad title and description to attract visitors to click on your ad. In the event that there are zero impressions, you should contact Bing support for assistance to investigate (which is a rare case).

What should I do if I'm still not getting any sales from my campaign?

There is no guarantee that all campaigns will turn out profitable so it is important to know where to draw the line so as to keep any losses to a minimum. A basic rule of thumb that I have been using is to run a campaign, while doing all the necessary tweaking, until spending exceeds twice the amount of commission per sale. For example, I am promoting a product that gives me a commission of $30 per sale. If I still do not receive a single sale after my advertising spending hits $60, I will proceed to stop the campaign and move on to promote another product.

Can I apply the direct linking strategy to other affiliate programs?

Of course you can! The concept is the same; you need to make more than what you invest in PPC!

Is it a worthwhile investment to join ClickBank University?

ClickBank University is a training program launched by ClickBank in 2014. I have personally enrolled in the program and found that most of the training is geared towards teaching you how to make money by creating products in ClickBank. If you want to become a product creator, you will find ClickBank University to be highly relevant. However if you are looking at making money through promoting ClickBank products, this program may not be suitable for you.

Do you have video tutorials for all the steps in this book?

This book is a simplified version of my bestselling ClickBank online course in Udemy. If you prefer to learn through watching my videos, you can join my online course. You only need to pay a one-time fee to receive lifetime access to all my existing and updated video lessons! If you're keen to enroll in my online course for the opportunity to interact with thousands of other like-minded students online, I have attached a special coupon code at the end of this book for you to enjoy the online course at an INCREDIBLE discount!

If I can't generate a stable income through direct linking, what strategy should I use then?

In all businesses (online and offline), contacts and network is your greatest asset! Similarly if you want to generate a good income through promoting ClickBank products, you should work on creating a list of subscribers and building up rapport with them through regular communication. When people like and trust you, they will buy what you recommend to them. Read on to discover how you can start building your list and create massive income for your future!

How to Create Long Term Income Leveraging ClickBank Products!

I have been in the Internet business since 2005 and year after year, despite the evolution of new technologies and companies, the most effective marketing channel for my online business is still email marketing – educating and recommending solutions to my own mailing list!

Making money as a ClickBank affiliate is no different. If you want to earn recurring income through promoting ClickBank products, you must build a group of subscribers that follow you, like you and trust you! With a list of loyal followers, that's when you will be able to make money anytime you recommend them a product!

There are a few principles that guide me in building my list and I would strongly recommend you to follow them as well to accelerate your success.

Build a List Based On Your Interest

I realize too many people jump into the make money online niche even though they do not have any relevant experience in this niche and they end up losing money!

I'm not going to ask you to go after the biggest market blindly. Instead, go with something that you have interest and knowledge in. For example, if you are a chef or you have an interest in cooking, you can start building a list of subscribers based on topics related to cooking. In fact, cooking is too general; it would be good if you can focus on a particular sub-niche, say 5-minute quick preparation meals for busy professionals.

Just remember one thing – never build a list based on a topic that you have no knowledge or interest in, because you'll need to communicate with your followers often and send them relevant tips and advice regularly. Bear this tip in mind; it will save you a lot of time and effort in the long run.

Build a List of Subscribers Based On a Niche, Not a Product

One common mistake most people make is to build their list around a product. This is not a viable approach because it is common for products to come and go. Imagine this, what if the product you choose now no longer exists a few months later, wouldn't that render all the hard work you put in to building your list redundant? Instead, you should build your list based on a niche. With that, you will be able to connect with your subscribers in many ways beyond just talking about the affiliate product that you are promoting. You can also send them useful information or resources to help them in that topic and build up your relationship with your audience.

In short, it is easy to get carried away if you put too much focus on a product alone, so always bring the attention back to you or the niche that you are in so that your subscribers know you more than the product. This way, they will start to remember you and trust you when you make any product recommendations to them in future!

Educate More Than You Sell

The key to success in email marketing is to educate more than you sell. You may be wondering why on earth do we need to do that since the job of an affiliate is to promote and sell ClickBank products! To the contrary, doing this right will only help you to get more sales in the long term. This may sound like a hard thing to do at the beginning but just bear this in mind for now – you have to first go slow before you start to make money fast!

In actual fact, a lot of successful Internet marketers do not make huge money overnight. It is accomplished through the process of building a sizeable mailing list overtime and keeping in regular contact with subscribers. As you continue to build trust with your contacts through the value that you provide, you will see amazing results for yourself. That's the time when conversions come in fast – once you send out an email with your recommendations about a product that you are promoting, sales happen!

But before your lead turns into your customer, there is work to be done. Always begin by educating your list; you need to give before you take. Follow these timeless principles and it will help you to get consistent results. In the next chapter, I will teach you how to start building your list by creating a squeeze page!

3 Minute Squeeze Page Secrets That No One Tells You! (Creating a Squeeze Page Without Domain and Hosting)

An effective approach to build your subscriber list is to capture leads through a squeeze page. Typically, you'll need a domain name and web hosting for that, but in line with the title of this book, I will show you a way to create a squeeze page easily *without* a website. Yes you don't need any domain or hosting at all! I've been teaching this method to my students – it's simple, cost-effective, and surprisingly not many people know it yet!

What exactly is a squeeze page? It is a simple landing page with the sole purpose of drawing visitors to opt-in to your mailing list so that you can capture their contact information and follow up with them.

To create a squeeze page without a domain and hosting, I'll recommend GetResponse30.com. Beyond just a tool for creating squeeze pages, it is the only one-stop email marketing platform (at the time of writing) that comes with both autoresponder *and* squeeze page capabilities. This means that you can create a squeeze page in GetResponse30.com itself (without the need for a domain and hosting) and the leads captured through the squeeze page will also be linked to the autoresponder where you can schedule follow-up emails to be sent to your subscribers automatically.

Previously, in order to create a squeeze page, I had to pay an additional $12 plus $100 every year to purchase a domain and hosting respectively. However after I discovered GetResponse30.com, I get to save on all these costs plus enjoy all the services I need for my email marketing (squeeze page, autoresponder) for only $15 a month!

To register yourself an account, just go to GetResponse30.com. They offer a free trial for the first 30 days and if you like it, you can continue to use their services for only $15 every month and you can choose to cancel your subscription anytime. (Note: GetResponse30.com is my affiliate link and I would appreciate if you could register for your account through this link. The small commission that I receive will help to keep the price of this book low.)

Once you have gotten your GetResponse30.com account, here is how you can use it to promote ClickBank products:

1. Select a product to promote in ClickBank (as explained in the first part of this book).
2. Create a squeeze page in GetResponse30.com.
3. Schedule follow-up emails to be sent to your subscribers in GetResponse30.com autoresponder.
4. Create a new ad campaign in Bing Ads to direct visitors to your squeeze page when they click on your ad.
5. After the visitor enters his/her contact information into the squeeze page, redirect them to the sales page of the ClickBank product that you are promoting.
6. Subsequently the subscriber will continue to receive your emails automatically based on the pre-scheduled messages in your autoresponder.

If you want to learn the exact steps to create a squeeze page in GetResponse30.com, do sign up for my mailing list so I can send you my tutorial videos!

Important Tips When Building Your List

In this chapter I want to share with you some important pointers about creating your squeeze page.

GetResponse30.com provides a wide range of ready-to-use templates that you can choose from. From the opt-in category, pick a template that has a clean, simple design. Avoid using complicated-looking templates as they distract the attention of your visitors and are generally less effective. Some of the good templates that I like to use for my campaigns are Deal of the week, Tick Tock and Arrows.

After you have selected a template to use, you can modify it further to suit your needs. For example you can replace wordings, delete or move elements around using drag and drop. Just make sure that the two most important fields – name and email – are kept there because your bottom line is to capture the contact information of your visitors.

Now comes the critical question: How do you get your visitors to give you their personal details willingly? Surely no one will give you their name and email for nothing so you must think about what you can offer them in exchange for their contact information. Here are some ideas on what you can give to your subscribers:

1. **Free ebook** - Some product creators in ClickBank provide affiliates with a rebrandable ebook that you can give away. This should be the first resource that you use for building your list.

2. **PLR ebook** - Alternatively you can purchase a Private Label Rights (PLR) ebook – which is relatively cheap – and give it away to your subscribers. I only use ebooks from ID PLR because they are one of the few websites around that provide high quality PLR products.

3. **Useful Tips & Newsletter** - If you do not have any information products to give away, you can offer to send useful tips and resources to your subscribers on a regular basis. This is a more tedious and time-consuming process but it is also the most effective way to build rapport with your subscribers, which is beneficial for conversions in the long term. For instance if you are promoting an ebook about LinkedIn, you can schedule weekly emails containing social media tips to be sent to your subscribers.

If you're giving away a digital product such as an ebook, one of the easiest way to manage delivery is to upload the file to Dropbox. Dropbox will then generate a special link that you can send to your subscribers directly for them to download the product.

In the next chapter I will share with you how you can send your free gift to the new subscriber automatically whenever someone signs up for your mailing list, and how to continue to build up rapport with them after that!

How to Build a List of Responsive Subscribers?

This chapter covers the core essentials of building relationships with your subscribers. A common mistake that most beginners make – which you must avoid at all costs – is to bombard your subscribers' mailboxes with nothing but promotional emails. This is a sure way to turn people off and doing this will only sabotage your chances of success.

Remember, building relationships is the key. It is about keeping in regular contact with your subscribers, engaging with them through your words, and constantly providing value through sharing useful information. When you start to establish yourself as a credible and knowledgeable figure, you are getting closer to making consistent sales in the near future. I have said this before and I will say it again – you must first go slow in order to make money fast!

Below you will learn how to write the first seven emails to be sent to every new person that subscribes to your mailing list. The entire process can be automated by pre-scheduling the emails in your GetResponse30.com autoresponder and the messages will be triggered accordingly by the system. Follow these tips and I am confident that you will be making money when your list hits 50 subscribers and more!

Email #1: Introduce yourself & make an impact! (Day 0)

A welcome email should be sent to every new subscriber immediately after he/she opts in to your list. In this first email, introduce yourself and thank the subscriber for joining your mailing list. If you promised your subscribers a free gift, this is also the time for you to provide them with detailed instructions on how to receive their gift (enclose download link for ebook, report, etc.). Finally tell them that they can expect to receive more useful resources from you in future!

Email #2: Give them a big benefit for subscribing! (Day 2)

You can schedule your second email to be sent out on day 2 after the person has subscribed. The sole purpose of this email is to give your new subscriber a surprise and there must be absolutely no selling in your message! It can be a gift or something as simple as a beneficial tip. If you run out of ideas on what to give, you can search online for relevant blog posts or articles and share it with them. They will appreciate you for the gesture! For example if hair loss is a topic of interest to your subscribers, you can google for 'hair loss prevention' and you will find plenty of practical tips that you can send to them!

Email #3: Share a testimonial! (Day 3)

On day 3, you can share a testimonial from someone who has tried the product that you are promoting. Just focus on sharing the testimonial and let your subscriber know that if they are interested, they can click on the link (your affiliate link) to find out more. Keep this email short and sweet!

Email #4: Give them more information relating to the affiliate product (Day 5)

In this fourth email, you can elaborate more about the product that you are promoting and list down the benefits of the product and why people should purchase it!

Email #5: Make an offer! (Day 7)

Day 7 is the time when you are ready to ask for a sale. One of the ways to create a sense of urgency for your subscribers to act immediately is to remind them that the offer is only available for a limited period of time, and that you do not know when the discounted price will be gone. Highlight the core benefit of the product again and urge them to take action now.

Email #6: Remind them of the offer! (Day 8)

This email should be sent one day after your previous email to remind your subscribers to take advantage of the offer while it still lasts. Please check to ensure that the product that you are promoting offers a discounted price on their sales page (which most ClickBank products would have).

Email #7: Share with them a useful video! (Day 10)

Around day 10 after the person has subscribed to your mailing list, you should kick start the educating process again. One thing that I like to do is to go to YouTube.com and look for interesting and relevant videos about the niche that I am in and share the link with my subscribers. This is something that can be done easily.

These first seven emails serve as a guide to help you get started and you should continue to work on scheduling more emails to connect with your subscribers on a regular basis. A general rule of thumb is that you should send out at least three educational emails before you attempt to promote a product to your list. This way, you will keep the number of people who unsubscribe from your list to a minimum.

On an ending note, having a list that is built around a niche allows you to multiply your earnings since you do not need to restrict yourself to promoting only ClickBank products to your subscribers! You are free to promote other non-ClickBank products so long as they are relevant to your audience. I often promote products from Amazon, iHerb (for health related products) or Udemy (online courses) to my list and you can do the same too!

Get Your US$100 Bonus Here!

As you may already be aware, I am the creator of the bestselling ClickBank online course in Udemy.com, Make Your First Real Dollar In ClickBank – With No Website.

I am happy to offer you a US$100 discount to my online course to thank you for your support. When you enroll in the online course, you will get:

- Over 20+ video lectures showing you how to make money with ClickBank!
- Up-to-date step-by-step videos that you can watch and follow on-demand 24/7!
- Interact and learn with more than 1000+ students online!
- Lifetime access to the entire course and future updates!

Access my ClickBank online course here:
https://www.udemy.com/making-money-with-clickbank/

To redeem your US$100 discount, enter the coupon code **amazon100**.

If you are not satisfied with my online course after signing up, you can request for a full refund within 30 days. I will honor any request.

I look forward to hear from you and do remember to join my mailing list so that you can get in touch with me!

I wish you all the best in your online business!

Further Resources

The following books have benefited me greatly and I hope you will find them useful as well. Enjoy the read!

1. How I Made My First Million on the Internet and How You Can Too!: The Complete Insider's Guide to Making Millions with Your Internet Business (by Ewen Chia)

2. Launch: An Internet Millionaire's Secret Formula To Sell Almost Anything Online, Build A Business You Love, And Live The Life Of Your Dreams (by Jeff Walker)

3. Get Rich Click!: The Ultimate Guide to Making Money on the Internet (by Marc Ostrofsky)

4. Ultimate Guide to Google AdWords: How to Access 100 Million People in 10 Minutes (by Perry Marshall)

5. Make a Fortune Promoting Other People's Stuff Online: How Affiliate Marketing Can Make You Rich (by Rosalind Gardner)

Printed in Great Britain
by Amazon